Publisher: International Federation of Tamils

First published October 2004

Copyright © IFT 2004

International Federation of Tamils
18 Rue des Pàquis,
1201 Geneva,
Switzerland.
Tel/Fax: +22 7320831
Email: infetamil@bluewin.ch
Email: ift@bluewin.ch

ISBN 0-646-43429-2

PRABHAKARAN

A Leader for All Seasons

This Album pays tribute to Prabhakaran,
a unique leader recognized as a legend in
his own time, who has restored the identity, integrity
and dignity of the Tamil Nation.

These are glimpses of the Man behind the Leader.

<u>Note</u>: Unless otherwise stated, all quotations are those of Prabhakaran.

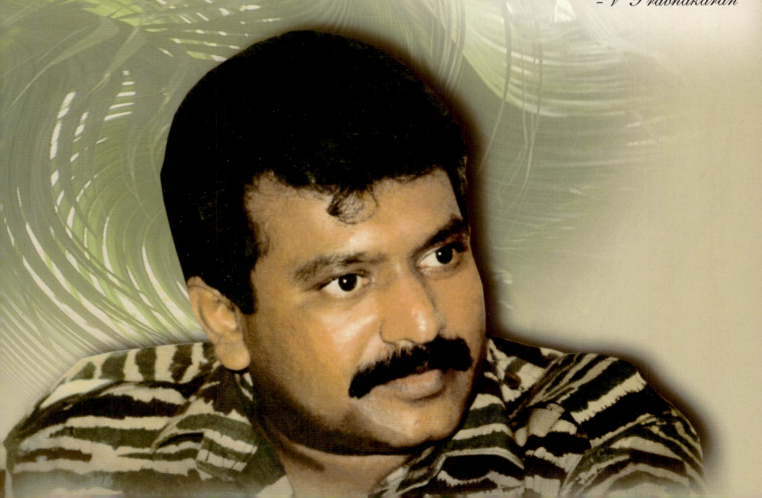

My ambition is to mould a new generation of youth who will be the architects of our future nation. This new generation will be scientific-minded, patriotic, honest, decent, heroic and possessed of a high sense of honour, self respect and dignity.

-V Prabhakaran

' *Kaarthikai Poo* '
(*Gloriosa Lily*)
National Flower of the Tamil Homeland

Prabhakaran

A Leader for All Seasons

The end of the Second World War spawned many liberation struggles in the Afro-Asia regions. Before the war, the European colonial powers, for administrative convenience, had amalgamated small countries and distinct regions into single administrative units with little consideration for their racial and cultural sensitivities and histories.

In the island of Sri Lanka too, the British amalgamated the Tamil and Sinhala Kingdoms - which until then had been treated as separate entities by the earlier Portugese and Dutch rulers - into one unit. When independence was granted in 1948, they handed the administration of the whole island to the Sinhalese in Colombo.

For decades, political and peaceful campaigns by the Tamil people for the restoration of their rights were answered with discrimination, intimidation and military oppression by the Sinhala forces. Ultimately the Tamils resorted to an armed liberation struggle. From this ultimate stand by the Tamils for their self preservation and dignity, rose the **Man of Destiny, Prabhakaran.**

From Visionary to Leader

Valvettithurai was a famous port of the last Jaffna Kingdom which existed from the early 13th Century to the 17th Century. It was here that Prabhakaran was born on 26th November 1954. His parents, Veluppillai of Thirumeniyar and Parvathy, daughter of Nagalingam of Pt. Pedro, were both from orthodox, affluent families. Veluppillai was a Lands Officer for the Sri Lankan Government. Prabhakaran was the youngest of their four children.

> *" I was brought up in an environment of strict discipline from childhood… Great store was laid by personal rectitude and discipline. My father set an example through his own personal conduct…"*

His education at Chithambara College in Valvettithurai was nonedescript and he was an average student. He loved history and read avidly of the lives of great leaders like Alexander the Great and Napoleon. The Indian nationalist leaders, Subhas Chandra Bose and Bhagat Singh, were to become sources of inspiration to him. It was the norm for children of affluent families in Jaffna to continue their education in English in preparation to go abroad or to join the Government Service. However, the young Prabhakaran was different.

He became highly sensitive to the harassment and intimidation of the Tamils by the Sinhala armed forces even as a child. The 1958 anti-Tamil riots left him deeply disturbed.

" ...I heard horrifying incidents of how our people had been mercilessly and brutally put to death by Sinhala racists. Once I met a widowed mother, a friend of my family, who related to me her agonizing personal experience of this racial holocaust. A Sinhala mob attacked her house in Colombo. The rioters set fire to the house and murdered her husband. She and her children escaped with severe burn injuries... When I heard such stories of cruelty, I felt a deep sense or sympathy and love for my people..."

As told to Anita Pratap,
Sunday Magazine, March 11-17 1984

The discriminatory policy of standardisation which deprived Tamils of fair university and employment opportunities angered him even as a Year 10 student. He and fellow students joined the Tamil Students Organisation (Thamil Maanavar Peravai).

Instead of addressing their grievances, the Government arrested and tortured these students. This only served to fuel the indignation of the young Prabhakaran.

In 1972, at the age of 17, he gathered his colleagues and formed the resistance movement, " Tamil New Tigers ", the members coming from friends and relatives. The Movement grew into an armed Liberation movement and changed its name on 5th May 1976 to the *Liberation Tigers of Tamil Eelam.*

Prabhakaran stressed adherence to a strict code of conduct as the main criteria for membership into the LTTE. When asked once who were his beacons, his reply was characteristic:

" Nature is my friend, Life my philosopher and History my guide."

History is full of tales of men who rose to meet the need of the time. Here was one such Man; the time of need had come for the Tamil people for such a man. Today, to his followers he is the inspiring object of devotion and respect, their **'Annai'**.

To the Tamil people in the north and east of Sri Lanka and to the hundreds of thousands of Tamils flung all over the globe, he is the unquestioned Leader, simply, their **'Thalaivar'**.

Prabhakaran aged 17

Speaking of formative influences on his character to N. Ram,
the then Associate Editor of 'The Hindu':

"*...From my boyhood, the struggle that attracted me most was the Indian freedom struggle. The role of Netaji attracted me very much... Subhas attracted me particularly... He became my special hero and some of his orations gripped me. For example, 'I shall fight for the freedom of my land until I shed my last drop of blood.' These words used to thrill me whenever they came to me. Then the story of Bhagat Singh fascinated me.*"

'The Hindu' Madras,
September 4th & 5th 1986

" We are standing on a righteous platform. Our struggle ideal is legitimate. Our people are entitled to self determination. They qualify for autonomy under international law."

TODAY...

Tamils at home and abroad have rallied behind the leadership of Prabhakaran who has achieved remarkable military victories and restored lost territory under Tamil control. He has established a de facto state with a unique administrative and judicial structure for the Tamil homeland.

The ability to defend territory coupled with the strength to recapture lost territory has given the Liberation Tigers the strength and confidence to negotiate a political settlement for their people. With this confidence, Prabhakaran initiated a unilateral ceasefire in December 2001. A peace process with Sri Lanka facilitated by the Government of Norway has been underway with a Memorandum of understanding signed in February 2002. A settlement however, is yet to be achieved.

The Tamil people have put their absolute trust in Prabhakaran as the only leader capable of leading them in war and peace. This was reinforced by the resounding victory of the LTTE backed Tamil National Alliance at the 2004 elections.

Signing of the Ceasefire Agreement February 2002

The Peace-mover

Prabhakaran has consistently and continually reiterated his desire for a political solution through peaceful means. His several attempts to find a negotiated solution to the ethnic conflict have not been grasped by the two major Sinhala political parties in the South which failing to realize the genuine desire of the Tamil leadership, have continued to pursue a military solution.

In November 2000 and again in November 2001, Prabhakaran initiated peace by declaring unilateral ceasefires. A Norwegian government-facilitated memorandum of understanding was signed with the new government of Prime Minister Ranil Wickremasinghe in February 2002. A political settlement, however, is yet to be negotiated. Yet again, due to the power struggle between the two major Sinhala political parties of Sri Lanka, it appears that history is about to repeat itself.

Prabhakaran has referred to this in his annual Heroes Day address in November 2003:

"… As a tragic drama without an ending, the Tamil ethnic conflict continues forever. Whenever the Party in power attempts to resolve the Tamil issue, the Party in Opposition opposes it and derails the effort. The mode of conflict continues even when the opposition becomes the ruling party and attempts reconciliation. This Sinhala political drama with its typical historical pattern has been staged regularly for the last 50 years. The directors of this bizarre drama are the two major Sinhala political parties. Though the main actors have been changing over time, the theme of the story is the same. The current political crisis in Colombo is an open enactment of this absurd drama…"

As facilitators of the Peace Process, Norwegian Foreign Minister Jan Petersen and Deputy Foreign Minister Vidar Helgesen are welcomed to the Tamil homeland - 15 May 2003.

The MGR-Prabhakaran bonhomie...

"… he became the blue-eyed boy of the Tamil Nadu Chief Minister.

Nobody could surmise what their relationship was like. 'It was some chemistry', said Panrutti S.Ramachandran… And the relationship lasted almost until MGR's death in December 1987, even after the IPKF cracked down on the LTTE. Others in Madras thought MGR saw in Prabhakaran the replica of the big screen hero that he himself was, fighting for a just cause..."

M. R. Narayan Swamy, 'Tigers of Lanka'
Vijitha Yapa Publications, Colombo 2004

With Chief Minister of Tamil Nadu, M. G. Ramachandran - 1984

" *...Though we stand today as a formidable force strengthened by manpower, firepower, moral power and people's power and have the military capability to liberate our homeland, we have not abandoned the path of peace. We want to resolve the Tamil conflict through peaceful means, through civilized methods, without recourse to a bloodbath and the destruction of life...*"

Heroes Day Speech 27-11-99

Following the Memorandum of Understanding, Generals of both the Armies meet to effect the opening of the famous A9 Highway - April 2002.

Prabhakaran has never wavered from his desire for peace with honour.

" *We are not opposed to peace, nor are we opposed to a resolution of the conflict by peaceful means. We want an authentic peace, a true, honourable, permanent peace; a condition in which our people can live with freedom and dignity in their own land without external coercion determining their own political life. We have grave doubts whether the forces of Sinhala-Buddhist chauvinism will allow such a peaceful life to the Tamil people.*"

Heroes Day Speech 27-11-96

European Union's Commissioner for External Relations, Mr Chris Patten, meets
Mr Prabhakaran - 26 November 2003

" *...We want the political negotiations to be held in an atmosphere of peace and normalcy, free from the conditions of war, military aggression and economic blockades. We are not stipulating any pre-conditions for peace talks. We are suggesting the creation of a climate of peace and goodwill to hold peace talks, a congenial environment in which our people must be free from the heavy burden of suffering imposed on them. We hold the view that political negotiations cannot be free, fair and just if the Government utlizes the military aggression on our soil and the restrictions imposed on the economic life of our people as political pressures...*"

Heroes Day Speech 27-11-98

Mr Prabhakaran receives Norwegian Ambassador, H.E. Jon Westborg - 6 April 2002.

" ...We wish to reiterate that peace talks should be held in a cordial peaceful atmosphere of mutual trust and goodwill with the assistance of international third party mediation. By peaceful atmosphere we mean a condition of normalcy characterised by cessation of hostilities, withdrawal of troops occupying Tamil lands and the absence of economic blockades..."

Heroes Day Speech 27-11-99

Ambassador Westborg and Mr Eric Solheim introduce the Scandinavian Ceasefire Monitoring Team - 6 April 2002.

" *...The Tamil national question, which has assumed the character of a civil war, is essentially a political issue. We still hold a firm belief that this issue can be resolved by peaceful means. If there is genuine will and determination on the part of the Sinhalese leadership there is a possibility for peace and settlement...*"

Heroes Day Speech 27-11-2000

With Mr Anton Balasingham, his Political Advisor, at the media conference - 10 April 2002.

" ...We are not enemies of the Sinhala people, nor is our struggle against them...

...We are well aware that this war has not only affected the Tamils but also affects the Sinhala people deeply. Thousands of innocent Sinhala youth have perished as a consequence of the repressive policies of the war mongering ruling elite. We are also aware that it is the Sinhala masses who are bearing the economic burden of the war. Therefore, we call upon the Sinhala people to identify and renounce the racist forces committed to militarism and war and to offer justice to the Tamils in order to put an end to this bloody war and to bring about permanent peace..."

Heroes Day Speech 27-11-2000

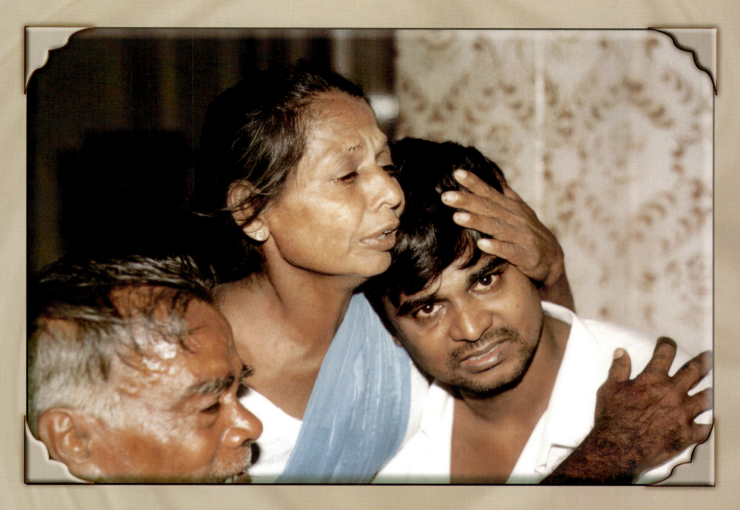

The parents of Sri Lankan prisoners of war were moved with gratitude and touched by the hospitality extended to them when the LTTE invited them to visit their sons.

" *Our organisation, as well as our people do not want war. We want peace and we want to resolve our problems through peaceful means. We are deeply committed to the peace process. It is because of our sincere commitment to peace that we are firmly and rigidly observing ceasefire. It is our organisation that took the initiative of declaring the cessation of hostilities unilaterally and observing peace for the last two years tolerating the provocative actions of the state's armed forces.*"

Heroes Day Speech 27-11-03

Mr Akashi, who has been appointed as Special Envoy to the Peace Process, is greeted by Mr Prabhakaran who presents him with a memento of the visit.

" *The determination of a people, support from the world community and a conducive environment dictate the victories of liberation strunggles.*"

" *Our people have melted in Sinhala racism, faces the atrocities of state terrorism, forever carried the cross of hazards and slept in the shadow of death.*"

In discussion with the Norwegian delegation.

" *When patriotism grips the conscience of a people it is then that a nation attains its unique national sovereignty.*"

" *Reforms to restore social equality and social justice can only be achieved by infusing changes to basic interactions in the social structure.*"

In discussion with Mr Chandrasekeran, Leader of the Upcountry Peoples Front - 14 April 2002.

" *The world community that raises its voice for the justice and human rights of people must raise its voice for our people who are begging for justice and peaceful resolution of their rights. This is a moral obligation.*"

" *From then to now, the Tamil struggle for liberation is a justified one. The stamp of justice is imbued in our non-violent and armed struggles. This morality has been the soul of our struggle.*"

With members of his Negotiating Team before they left for the Peace talks in Thailand - October 2002

" The Tamil freedom struggle is a struggle for self determination. It is a struggle for political freedom and right to decide our destiny."

(News Feature) Mr. Rauf Hakeem, leader of the Sri Lanka Muslim Congress (SLMC) and a delegation from his party flew to the LTTE-held town of Kilinochchi on Saturday morning for discussions with an LTTE delegation headed by the movement's leader, Mr. Vellupillai Pirapaharan.

Mr. Hakeem said the talks with the LTTE leader were friendly and productive. The three and a half hours of discussion centred around several problems faced by Muslims in the Northeast, he said.

Tamilnet - 20 April 2002

Meeting with the Leader of the Muslim Congress, Mr Rauf Hakeem, and other members - 13 April 2002.

Jyotindra Dixit, India's Foreign Secretary, in 'Assignment Colombo':

"...Prabhakaran's success in gathering around him senior advisers with diverse political, administrative and technological capacities, which contributed to effective training of his cadres, optimum utilisation of the military equipment which he had, and the structuring of an efficient command and control system."

J. N. Dixit in 'Assignment Colombo'
Konarak Publishers, 1998

Sharing a light moment with members of his negotiation team.

" It is when we share the hardships of our people that they accept us and bond with us."

Mr.Thondaman, CWC leader met reporters at the Katunayake International Airport lounge Sunday afternoon on his return from LTTE held town of Killinochchi in the Vanni region.

"CWC and LTTE have agreed to work together for the right of self-determination of Tamils. The CWC would support all steps taken by the LTTE in its struggle in this regard."

Tamilnet - 15 April 2002

With Mr Arumugam Thondaman, Leader of the Ceylon Workers Congress which represents the workers of Indian Tamil origin - 14 April 2002.

" Politics is not about ruling the people, it is about serving the people."

(News Feature) *"The Tamil people voted for you on the basis of the principles of Tamil nationalism. You should understand their feelings and work to realise their aspirations. Love for one's country comes from one's love for home, family, village and region. In this sense I encouraged love for one's region, as it is necessary to strengthen a liberation struggle. But it is dangerous when the affection for one's region is exploited for selfish motives"*, said Mr. Velupillai Pirapaharan, speaking to 22 MPs of the Tamil National Alliance at the LTTE's political division headquarters in Kilinochchi .

Tamilnet - 20 April 2004

Meeting with Tamil Parliamentarians of the Tamil National Aliance following the resounding election victory in April 2004.

'Thalaivar' The Leader

"…To arouse entirely new attitudes and a new creative type of followers is the supreme height of leadership. To arouse unsuspected possibilities and originalities in other persons makes for the greatest leadership. The techniques are often those of the superior teacher, case-worker, parent, who challenge and give heavy responsibilities, who set forth unique opportunities, who make the impossible seem possible, who by deed or word arouse their followers to superhuman effort…"

Emory Borgadus in 'Leadership and Attitudes'
Sociology and Social Research Journal

The success of any liberation organization relies solely on resolute leadership. Prabhakaran's vision for his people has never once wavered. He set about building a new order for the Tamils with a single-minded, totally dedicated, inspiring leadership which has won open admiration from his people, as well as grudging compliments from his detractors.

" I named the movement 'Liberation Tigers' since the tiger emblem had deep roots in the political history of the Tamils, symbolising Tamil patriotic resurgence."

" My political goal is to build a society thriving in social justice and democracy."

" Our people should be admired. They should be honoured. The contribution of our people to the Liberation struggle is invaluable. I would say that those sympathisers and supporters who have continued to provide moral support to the struggle are great human beings."

As a leader Prabhakaran has shown himself to be an astute and intelligent military man, inspiring in his philosophy of nationalism, gratifying in his compatriotism, and above all, tender in his compassion for those who suffer pain and loss.

" I feel proud of my people, my nation and my liberation movement."

Adele Balasingham, on her first meeting with Prabhakaran in 1979:

" Mr Prabhakaran's young face was clear and bright and his huge black eyes penetrating. Indeed, one gets the feeling that he is peering right through to your soul and it is this depth in his eyes which mirrors his mind and thinking too."

Adele Balasingham in 'The Will to Freedom'
A Fairmax Publication

With late Col. Shankar and the pet leopard - Manalaru Camp 1989

" The literature and artistic creations must awaken patriotism and valour in our people to struggle for our ideals. These creations must help strengthen our struggle for freedom."

" The yearning for freedom is the breath that keeps us alive. This great power is what makes human history."

Camp Photograph - Manalaru 1988

"…Even his enemies concede that Mr. Prabhakaran is a formidable leader. Despite the toll of the civil war, he appears to retain the support of the majority of Tamils in northern and eastern Sri Lanka, the area which the Tigers claim as the Tamil homeland…"

Economist, March 6, 1993

" Our literature should depict our struggle. They should truly present the oppression that is prevalent in every walk of our people's lives."

The Family Man

" Men and women must respect each other's freedom and equality to share the responsibilities in family life to work for a better society. This understanding will alleviate various differences and gender prejudices."

"After all, Prabhakaran is not a small man. He is the leader, a charismatic leader of the LTTE. His life is very precious. And a very simple man. No bullshit about him. His wife lived with three saris - one she wore, one she washed and one was ready to wear. That is all. They never drank Coca-Cola. They offered us Coca-Cola, but never drank it themselves. They drank that *goliwala* soda."

Major General Harkirat Singh
Indian Peace Keeping Force 1987

With wife Mathivathani

Marriage with Mathivathani

Early days of their marriage, very austere but beautiful.

"...She wore a printed wrinkle-free sari and a modest blouse. She seemed gentle and domesticated. At his request, she handed him their son. 'His name' said Pirabhakaran looking down at his infant, 'is Charles Antony.'

Charles Antony had been Pirabhakaran's right-hand man, his trusted lieutenant and his oldest friend... In early July 1983, Charles was killed in a military operation.

When Pirabhakaran named his firstborn after his loyal right-hand man, he named his daughter after his slain personal bodyguard and his younger son after his brother in law who was killed in an encounter with the IPKF..."

Anita Pratap in 'Island of Blood'
Penguin India Publication 2001

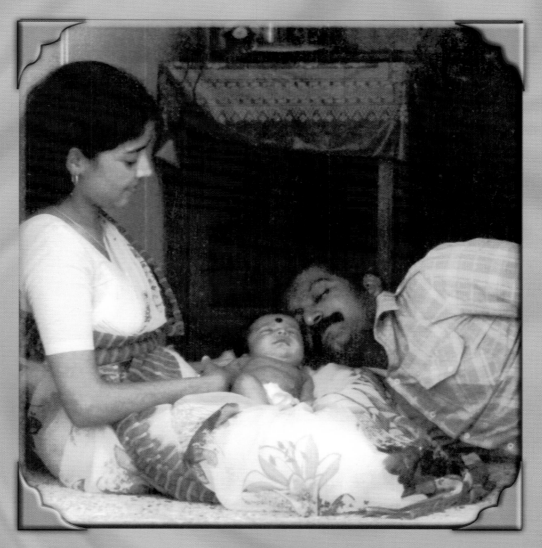

With his wife Mathy and firstborn child, Charles Antony.

The playful father at home with his children Charles and Dhwarka. For Prabhakaran who adores children, time with his own children is a rarity. Every moment spent with the family is therefore precious.

For his children too, the times with their father are very special.

The Compatriot

The leader and the man are one with the people he leads. Ever conscious that it is the fighters and the people who give life to a movement of liberation, Prabhakaran has always identified himself with them.

" ...I noticed the comaraderie between Prabhakaran and the other LTTE leaders. The bonhomie was remarkable - they would giggle and whisper among themselves like schoolboys in a locker room. I assumed war and the difficult years had helped them bond in a unique way. Prabhakaran was one of the boys, chatting and joking in an endearingly affectionate way..."

Anita Pratap in 'Island of Blood'
Penguin India Publication 2001

Early Camp Photograph - Manalaru 1988

"...I realized then that loyalty begets loyalty. The reason LTTE cadres are so loyal to Pirabhakaran is because his loyalty to them is legendary."

Anita Pratap in 'Island of Blood'
Penguin India Publication 2001

The Leader and the man are one with the people he leads.

" He believed, and most military men would probably agree with him, that discipline was essential to morale and high performance of cadres. His high moral character, to the point of puritanism, was the other quality for which he was well-known… He views exemplary behaviour in personal life as a crucial factor if a leader is to retain authority. Neither of these traits of his personality and behaviour has waned over the years."

Adele Balasingham in 'The Will to Freedom'
A Fairmax Publication

With Anton and Adele Balasingham - Manalaru, 1989

The Military Leader

" The world may sympathize when our people are slaughtered by Sinhala chauvinists. They may condemn, they may shed tears. But we must realize that protecting our people and securing their liberation is our own responsibility."

Today the LTTE led by Prabhakaran has attained the status of a conventional army, recognized as the most disciplined, inspired, incorruptible and resolute force the world has seen in modern times. This was not achieved simply. Prabhakaran nurtured the sense of righteous indignation and yearning for dignity in the hearts of his followers and in a miraculously short time turned them into a formidable fighting force. This can only happen when the leader himself displays the qualities required in his followers.

" Tamil fighters are forged from discipline, nationalism and worship of their leader. There is Prabhakaran, the incorruptible, who refuses to deviate from his goal of Eelam despite military pressure from India, despite offers of money and power from Colombo and New Delhi that turned the heads of less resolute Tamil leaders."

'Inside the Tiger Mind'
Time Magazine, Asian edition
September 16, 1991

Military photograph 1999 - Prabhakaran's unique leadership skills have been amply demonstrated in his delegatory excellence in military, political and administrative areas.

On being asked by Anita Pratap as to why he believed an armed struggle was the solution for the Tamils in Sri Lanka:

" The shocking events of the 1958 racial riots had a profound impact on me when I was a school boy... I felt a deep sense of sympathy for my people. A great passion overwhelmed me to redeem my people from this racist system. I strongly felt that armed struggle was the only way to confront a system which employs armed might against unarmed, innocent people."

Anita Pratap : Sunday Magazine
March 11-17 [th] 1984

Early training photograph taken in India - 1984

" ...The LTTE's emergence as the most dominant and effective politico-military force representing Tamil interests was due to the following factors:

First, the character and personality of its leader, V.Prabhakaran, who is disciplined, austere and passionately committed to the cause of Sri Lankan Tamils' liberation. Whatever he may be criticised for, it cannot be denied that the man has an inner fire and dedication and he is endowed with natural military abilities, both strategic and tactical. He has also proved that he is a keen observer of the nature of competitive and critical politics. He has proved his abilities in judging political events and his adroitness in responding to them..."

Jyotindra Dixit, India's Foreign Secretary
in his book 'Assignment Colombo'
Konarak Publishers, 1998

Early training camp photograph - 1985

" Our struggle has faced many challenges but basically it is because of our strength of purpose that we were able to progress in our journey."

Marshall R Singer, Ph.D. Professor of International and Intercultural Affairs, Graduate School of Public and International Affairs - University of Pittsburgh:

" ...The Tigers are ruthless and authoritarian but they are not corrupt – they don't tolerate stealing, bribery or rape, things other armies are famous for. In fact they are perceived as being single-minded in their defence of Tamils..."

Statement before the US Congress Committee on International Relations, Sub-committee on Asia and the Pacific Hearing on Sri Lanka, November 14th 1995

Training Camp Manalaru - 1989

" Words cannot adequately describe the perils, pain and sufferings faced by our fighters in this long and dangerous war for Tamileelam."

The Inspiration . . .

" Life is precious. But more precious than life is our freedom , our rights and our dignity."

Tamil History will acknowledge that in a relatively short time Prabhakaran has mobilised the Tamil People to feel as one for the liberation of their land. He has inspired a thirst for freedom that has sustained his people through untold hardship and misery.

" It is in the end, Prabhakaran whose will binds the Tigers. His followers call him *Annai*, or elder brother, and talk of him with wide-eyed awe, their only fear the possibility that they might let him down. 'He is mother, father and god all rolled into one,' says a guerrilla named Sunil. Government soldiers tell of a badly wounded female Tiger they captured at Elephant Pass. Her dying words were not a call for her mother, but for '*Annai, Annai.*"

'Inside the Tiger mind'
Time Magazine, Asian edition
September 16 1991

Training Camp 1989 - Prabhakaran has developed this organization which had its humble beginnings with one revolver, today to a fully-fledged conventional army.

" The wheels of History are turned by the rise of a People hungry for freedom."

" ...I have a high regard for the LTTE for its discipline, dedication, determination, motivation and technical expertise... I was left with the impression that the LTTE was the expression of popular Tamil sentiment and could not be destroyed, so long as that sentiment remained..."

Lt. General S.C. Sardesh Pande
in "Assignment Jaffna" 1992

1989 Photo - Initially local resources were used to produce small arms and later the organisation amassed heavy weaponry from the enemy.

" It was not easy to choose the liberation idealogy. History has forced this on us. History has left us no other alternative than seeking freedom."

" Victory in a war does not depend on manpower or weapons. Firm determination, valour and love of freedom are the factors that decide victory in a war. Our fighters and our people are full of these."

Economist, March 6, 1993

Inspecting the haul of automatic weapons from the captured Sri Lankan army camp in Mandai Thivu- 1995.

" *If we are to spearhead our liberation to protect our people from genocide, we must evict the enemy who is occupying our land. This is dependent on our careful planning and the unanimous participation of our people.*"

" *It is easy to fathom our enemies and their motives, but traitors have masks and they are the puppets of our enemy. Our people must be wary of these dangerous traitors who for their own benefits will not hesitate to betray their race.*"

Planning the defence of his people - 1999

" As long as there is injustice, oppression and people without freedom in this world, freedom struggles will be an inevitable reality."

" The valour of our fighters and the support from our people, gave us the great strength to dare a great power."

Inspecting the artillery acquired during the capture of Elephant Pass Army camp - April 2000.

*" The long lost Tamil tradition of valour has been revived.
A whirlwind has blown to wipe oppression out, hitherto trodden
Tamil man has risen as a mountain. Hitherto oppressed and
chained the Tamil nation has awakened from its slumber."*

*" The thirst for freedom comes from a deep rooted yearning
within the human soul."*

" It is might that determines today's World Order."

Jyotindra Dixit, India's Foreign Secretary in 'Assignment in Colombo':

" ...another factor (of the LTTE) is the cult and creed of honesty in the disbursement and utilisation of resources. Despite long years spent in struggle, the LTTE cadres were known for their simple living, lack of any tendency to exploit the people and their operational preparedness..."

Assignment Colombo, by J N Dixit,
Konarak Publishers, 1998

Defence experts acknowledge that Prabhakaran's army is one of the most disciplined and dedicated Liberation armies in the world.

" *The Sinhala military cannot break the resolve and determination of the Liberation Tigers. We are possessed of great moral, unique idealistic resolve and selflessness.*"

" *In History no freedom struggle was won merely by a movement alone. Only when it is backed by the people that it matures to become a mass movement.*"

" We have the strength, confidence and the resolve to fight to win our liberation."

" Geographically the security of Tamileelam is linked with the Sea. It is imperative that we have a naval force to defeat the sea-borne enemy to protect our coast as well as retain our territory on land."

Today, the Sea Tiger Division is a formidable Naval Force.

" It is the integrity, personal discipline and exemplary life style of our fighters which have earned the admiration of our people."

" As long as we have the conviction of our ideals, the resolve based on that conviction, and the fire from that resolve, we will continue in our idealistic journey to victory."

Inspects the guard of honour by the Tamil Eelam Naval force.

Honouring the Martyrs

Most often the Fallen in any war are remembered and honoured after the war. In the Liberation Struggle of Tamileelam, Prabhakaran initiated the remembrance and honour of the Fallen Heroes even in the midst of war and 27th November each year is celebrated as Heroes Day.

" Our liberation movement pays highest respect and reverence to our martyrs for their supreme sacrifice. We honour our martyrs as national heroes, as creators of the history of our national struggle. We commemorate our heroes and erect them memorials so that their memories should remain forever in our hearts. It has become a popular norm to bury our martyrs with honour, erect stone monuments for them and venerate these war cemeteries as holy places of tranquillity. The practice of venerating heroic martyrdom has become an established tradition in our society."

Heroes Day Speech, 27-11-97

27 November is Heros Day - Homage to the fallen martyrs who have sacrificed 'their todays' for 'our tomorrows'.

" My heart breaks when I lose my dear comrades, the cadres that I have nurtured and loved, my trusted lieutenants who have fought beside me. But I do not let these deter me; these only further strengthen my resolve to achieve my goal."

" Amazing sacrifices and magnificent offerings never seen in world history have transpired in our homeland."

" Our Martyrs are immortal, they are the sculptors of our freedom.
They have sown the great seed of yearning for freedom in our land."

Prabhakaran's Fast

Jyotindra Dixit, India's Foreign Secretary, in 'Assignment Colombo':

"… In a surprise move, the Tamil Nadu police was instructed to capture all the communication equipment of Tamil militant groups, especially the LTTE. This was done and Prabhakaran went on a fast.

This generated tension in Tamil Nadu, with everybody disclaiming responsibility for having taken the initiative to clip the wings of the LTTE. Minister Chidambaram, who was in charge of security, came out with a statement that the action was taken without consulting the Central Government. Tamil Nadu Government was annoyed with this and returned the equipment to Prabhakaran, persuading him to break his fast."

J. N. Dixit in 'Assignment Colombo'
Konarak Publishers, 1998

Explaining the reasons for embarking on his hunger strike to the well wishers and Indian politicians who visited him in Madras - 1986

August 1987 - Visibly dismayed Prabhakaran, when he returned from his meeting after discussing the Indo Sri Lanka Accord with Prime Minister Rajiv Gandhi.

4 August 1987 - The historic Suthumalai meeting, where on his return from New Delhi, Prabhakaran addressed his people who had gathered in to hear him.

His clear message to them became famous:

" The contours of our struggle may change but our ideals will remain the same."

Theleepan's fast

Demanding the full implementation of the Indo Lanka accord, Theleepan, a trusted Lieutenant, embarked on a fast which lasted 12 days. He attained martyrdom on the 12th Day.

"…Then the Thileepan fast happened. We tried our best. I went and tried to meet him. LTTE chaps told me, 'General, the people's emotions are so high that if you appear on the scene they might create a problem'. They asked me to stay there. I wanted to go and tell him, Give up. How will he give up? 'Unless the assurances given by the Prime Minister of India are fulfilled I am not giving up', he said. I kept requesting the High Commissioner, 'Come and meet, come and meet, come and meet.' He dragged his feet, he delayed it, he didn't come. Finally he came when the man was dead. We should have saved his life, one life…"

Major General Harkirat Singh, 1997 interview,

Rediff.com Indian website

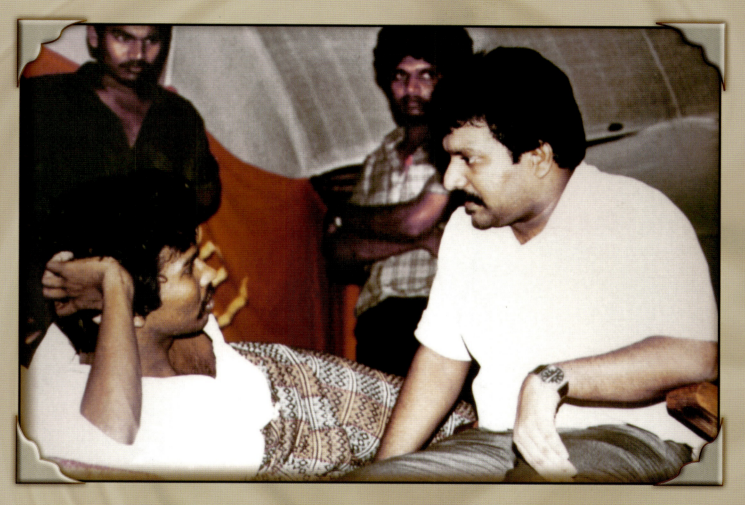

September 1987 - With Theleepan on the second day of his fast.
Theleepan attained matyrdom on the 12th day.

Col. Kittu, another trusted Leiutenant martyred when returning with a peace proposal from the Quaker Foundation. He was surrounded by the Indian Navy in International waters off Sri Lanka in January 1993. He refused to surrender and took his life.

" *The demise of a freedom fighter is not an ordinary event. It is a historic event that gives birth to a unique ideal. In fact a freedom fighter never really dies The flame of his ideals never die. This idealistic fire becomes a historical energy that ignites others. This awakens the soul of a nation.*"

January 1993 - A grief stricken Prabhakaran is comforting the mother of Col. Kittu.

" The history of our great freedom struggle is written with the blood, sweat and tears of our martyrs."

" Liberation is a journey through a river of fire. Immersed in this sacrificial fire, our martyrs have given their precious lives for our liberation."

The Visionary Nation Builder

" I am all afire to build up a nation - that is the life-ideal I have set for myself. The future generation is the foundation for the nation we hope to build. Therefore I consider bringing up the future generation and moulding its character and ideals as important as building up the nation."

History has seen successful leaders in all walks of life but they excelled only in one area or another. Prabhakaran is unique in that he is a warrior, protector, carer, family man and remarkable as a nation builder.

Amidst planning the defence of the Tamil territory, providing for his destitute people through a government economic blockade, Prabhakaran also was committed to building a nation. He envisioned a nation completely liberated, not only of army occupation but free also of the evils of the society.

During the five years of his administration (1990-1995) of the Jaffna peninsula, a society devoid of caste, religion and gender bias was built.

" As long as my people are behind me, I am prepared to face any new challenge."

" I wish to build a society of Tamileelam consisting of equality, justice and righteousness. I will not permit dishonest and devious administrators to destroy this new idealistic social order."

Seldom, if ever, rises a leader who acts and thinks of peace-time reforms and setting-up of rehabilitation institutions in a time of war. Prabhakaran has had the vision and the care to do just that. Little is known or commented upon this aspect of the Tamil Leader. The institutions instigated by him have gone far in meeting the needs of the refugees, children who have lost their parents, women traumatised by the evils of war, the physically crippled, and the old in a manner not seen in any war situation before.

As part of nation building, he encouraged and nurtured education for his people, pre-planned rehabilitation and programmes for people displaced due to war and long term planning for environmental protection and development. He honoured educationalists and academics in the Tamil homeland and abroad who contributed to the development and preservation of their respective fields.

Opening of the new Police Headquarters in Killinochchi - 2003

" Freedom is a national obligation. Everyone should bear responsibility. Every one has to share the hardships arising from a national tragedy. To let only the poor in the society to bear this is sacrilege to our nation."

" We Tamils are a structured race. Historically we have lived as a nation. We are living as a nation. We will continue to live as a nation."

All transactions are effected through Tamileelam Bank established as part of the infrastructure. A important function is the assistance rendered to the war affected families in self employment projects.

Sencholai Girls' Home and Kantharuban Boys' Home

" Please don't call it an orphanage. Orphans are those children
who have no one to care for them."

This is the over-all care-motto of both the children's homes. The motivation of Prabhakaran is that we cannot lose a generation. We have to take them safely through the war years so that they can take their rightful place in the society in the times of peace.

" They (the children) have lost their parents not their identity."

Children go through the basic disciplines and demands of living together. They are trained for vocations and an equal opportunity is provided for them to sit for all the public examinations. The successful students are a testimony to the 'equal opportunity for all' principle governing Prabhakaran's insistence on setting up such homes.

" Children are our Nation's future wealth. That is why I pay special attention to them."

2003 - Surrounded by happy youngsters during a visit to the Kantharuban Boys Home

1994 - With Children of Sencholai.

" I do not want to leave the burden of our freedom struggle to the next generation.
They must reap the benefit of our hard work."

Sharing the joys of children who have been donated a toy car by a well-wisher.

Rehabilitation Needs

" Our fighters have relinquished their families, their education, their future, the pleasures of their youth, for the liberation of their people. It is the Sinhala state terrorism that has driven our youth to the struggle."

Since 1990, when Prabhakaran encouraged Tamils to study prostheses techniques wherever they could (Germany especially), the White Pigeon Prosthetic Centre has been caring for and fixing artificial limbs for those maimed by war or land-mine accidents.

Using local materials, like wood and aluminium the prosthetic centre has valiantly endeavoured to fit out the maimed to the best of their ability.

" The Tamils cannot wait for an indifferent world to care about the needs of our war-torn Tamil Homelands; we need to help ourselves."

This has always been the attitude Prabhakaran encouraged in his people.

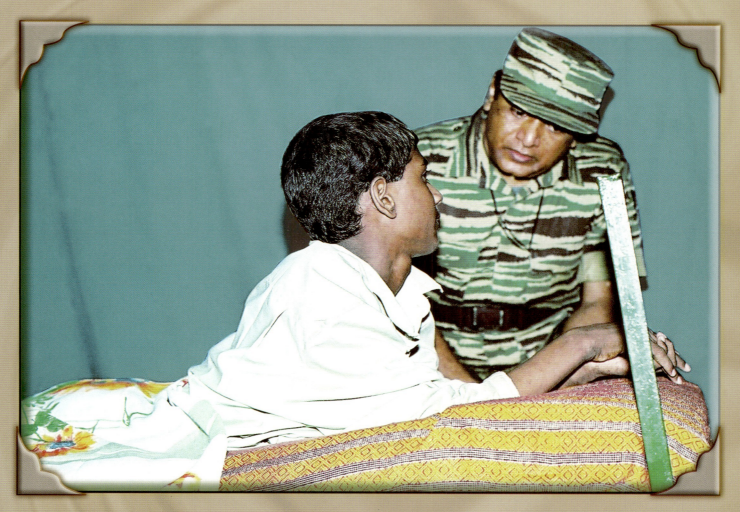

Discussing the rehabilitation of a fighter who is paralysed from waist down.

*" The longstanding sufferings, death and destruction and the
tears of our people do not appear to have touched the hearts of
the Buddhist Sinhala nation."*

One of the remarkable achievements of Prabhakaran as a leader is his ability to think
of the needs of rehabilitation in a comprehensive and lucid manner. Whereas, in most
war situations rehabilitation especially for women is hardly a thought, Prabhakaran
has instigated the establishment of various homes for the rehabilitation and assistance
for women.

The needs have been thought about very clearly and each institution serves a particular
group: bereft mothers, mentally disturbed women, young women capable of being
trained in specific vocations, disabled and so on. This is sophisticated rehabilitation
social thinking, seen more in times of peace rather than during war. Today, these many
homes in Eelam are a credit to Prabhakaran as a social thinker.

Discussing braille and other rehabilitation facilities with the vision impaired female cadres.

" Law and order are important components of civil administration. Justice should be administered by persons of impeccable honesty, integrity, discipline and exemplary character."

"A unique mind is important to analyse and judge an issue. A mind that is honest and not selfish, beyond personal preferences, beyond emotional attachments."

Officiating at the Graduation Ceremony of the Tamileelam Law College.

" Scholars, artists and academics cannot distance themselves from our historic struggle for liberation which has spread through all levels of our existence."

" When the Language, Culture and Arts develop and prosper, it strengthens the social structure of a nation. The society and its inter-relations are refined to reach sophistication."

In 1995 Prabhakaran felicitated and bestowed 'Mamanithar' award on Late Professor Thurairajah, Vice Chancellor of the Jaffna University, for his services to the Tamil community.

" *Our society should be a self-sufficient, self-dependent society.
I envisage a democratic government by which people rule themselves.
In this new society the working masses must have social equality.*"

" *Our struggle has faced many challenges but basically it is because
of our strength of purpose that we were able to progress on our
journey.*"

During a visit to the new Catering School, established to facilitate vocational training.

" It is only when the masses deeply feel patriotism that a nation achieves unique supremacy. It is a people with this unique supremacy who are qualified to govern themselves."

" Any race that rises for freedom must be economically self sufficient. Only such a people can enjoy freedom."

Electronic workshops for cadres to learn a vocation. Prabhakaran insists on concurrent educational, vocational or skills training to enable cadres to integrate in the society.

" I applaud the Tamil working class who bear the burden of the freedom struggle on one shoulder and the economic burden on the other."

" Self sufficiency in economy is the prime need for our nation. This is imperative for self governance."

Felicitating and rewarding farmers who have toiled to sustain the self sufficiency in agriculture.

Women and Liberation

" Within our struggle, we have revolutionized the women's liberation as never before in the history of the Tamils."

They say that one of the ways you assess a nation is by its attitude to women. The revolution that has taken place in the thinking of the Tamils is not limited to politics alone. Tamil women have undergone a revolution in the last two decades that is a credit to the thinking of the Leader. As one of the major reforms, the abolishment of the dowry system should receive special mention.

"Eventually, on the instructions of Mr. Prabhakaran, the LTTE lawmakers (the Justice Department) formulated new laws pertaining to the practice of dowry, upholding the property rights of women and abolishing the practice of cash donations to the relatives of the bridegroom. The most significant aspect of the new law was the removal of the ancient code that gave the husband control over his wife's property."

Adele Balasingham in 'The Will to Freedom.'
A Fairmax Publication

Inspects a guard of honour by the Tamil Eelam Women Police force.

" Whatever improvements are made to our world, Women's liberation will not become possible until and unless men consciously change their perceptions and attitudes."

"The struggle against male chauvinism is not a struggle against men but a struggle against the ignorance of man."

" *I would proudly say that the birth, growth and accomplishments of the Women's Brigade is one of the greatest achievements of our movement.*"

" *Dominance is not gender based. Humanity goes beyond gender. Humanity is common for men and women.*"

" *Women's subjugation is a complicated social issue. This is a cultural injustice that has infected our society for centuries. Our movement has resolved to uproot this social inequity.*"

With the female Cadres of the Media and Film Unit.

" In a real sense, the LTTE is like a large family. Many Jaffna people have relatives in the Tigers, and call them 'our boys'. Their monkish disciplines are admirable, if austere; no smoking, no drinking, no marriage until a certain age and number of years of service. They have revolutionized the role of women in Jaffna, giving them equality, as fighters, and striving to eliminate the dowry and caste systems."

Julian West, in the 'Passage to Jaffna'
Asiaweek magazine, March 8, 1991.

With his wife Mathi, participating in a wedding ceremony of one of his Commanders.

Seen only as the leader of a small armed rebel group a few years ago, Prabakaran is today, acknowledged by the world as the leader of a people with an ancient history and rich culture. The Tamils value Prabakaran as a historical figure who has brought about a revolution among the Tamil people, restoring dignity & self respect in their struggle for peace with justice.